Socialism Is Evil

The Moral Case Against Marx's Radical Dream

Justin T. Haskins

www.henrydearborn.org

Contents

Acknowledgments

While other children grew up hearing bedtime stories about monsters and faraway fantasy adventures, as a young boy in rural New Hampshire, my father would tuck me in at night as he told the legendary tales of men like John Adams, Thomas Jefferson, and George Washington. Through those stories, I learned to question everything with boldness, as well as the importance of individual liberty, servant leadership, and honor. Dad, this book is for you.

Socialism Is Evil

The Moral Case Against Marx's Radical Dream

Introduction

When most Americans hear the word "socialism," they usually think, depending on their political ideology, of one of the following commonly used descriptions: (1) a Scandinavian paradise full of happy, smiling, wealthy, and educated families who couldn't be more pleased with their well-functioning governments, or (2) a Venezuelan-style hellscape in which people fight to the death at grocery stores over the country's last remaining roll of toilet paper and kill zoo animals to feed their starving families.

As is often the case, the reality is that most people's experiences with socialism rests somewhere between those extreme points. In fact, most modern "socialist" societies only socialize certain aspects of their economies and rarely impose the sort of authoritarianism commonly found in many of the socialist countries that emerged in the first 70 years or so of the twentieth century.

The debate over the benefits and harms of socialism almost always devolves to a point in which opposing sides rely almost exclusively on caricatures to prove their arguments. For many who support or are sympathetic to socialism, every capitalist is a racist, white, wealthy, greedy businessperson who spends his Saturdays laughingly smoking cigars while dumping toxic waste into a river that feeds groundwater used by a nearby orphanage for special-needs kids.

Similarly, all socialists have become jackboot-wearing stormtroopers that dream of instituting an authoritarian society that looks more like North Korea than it does Sweden.

When data are presented in discussions of socialism, they also usually focus on extremes and fail to present a fair picture of what's really happening. Both sides cherry-pick evidence that best illustrates their points, and in the end, people genuinely curious about socialism are left with more questions than answers about collectivist governments.

As the title of this book clearly shows, I believe socialism is highly immoral. In fact, I believe it's one of the evilest economic systems ever devised. But unlike many who often discuss this topic, I don't believe socialism is immoral because it creates poverty. I do think a society attempting to impose socialism inevitably ends up with those problems in the long run, but the fear of economic inefficiencies is not the basis of the primary objection to socialism presented in this book.

The main reason I oppose socialism is because regardless of the outcomes a socialized country might experience, I believe a socialist system *requires* certain freedoms to be eliminated—freedoms so essential to humanity that they ought to be considered inalienable human rights. This view is incredibly important, because if I'm correct, the economic outcomes of a socialist model should be considered largely irrelevant in debates over socialistic systems.

I believe the evidence is overwhelming that attempts to implement socialism, given enough time, do not produce healthier, safer, happier societies than models that embrace individual liberty and free markets. But, as this book will show, even if such an ideal model could be developed, it wouldn't persuade me one bit, because such a system would still be immoral and deprive people of their most important freedoms.

Chapter One of this book examines what socialism is and how it works and discusses the differences between the socialism of philosophers like Karl Marx and Friedrich Engels and the modern "socialist" systems commonly found in Europe.

Chapter Two examines whether the advanced socialist system advocated by Marx and his ideological descendants is possible.

Chapter Three presents the primary argument of this book: Socialism is highly immoral, regardless of the outcomes socialist economies provide, and thus it should be rejected in the United States and everywhere else in the world. It also briefly explains how to define "evil" in the modern West, which has largely rejected a traditional understanding of the term.

Chapter Four, titled "European-Style Socialism," outlines many of the moral problems found in modern "mixed-socialist" societies, including Canada and many European countries.

Chapter Five answers several objections commonly made by socialists against those who argue socialism is extremely immoral.

Despite socialists' failures throughout the twentieth century, millions of Americans have in recent decades bought into the wildly idealistic fantasy that Marx's socialism can be effectively implemented in the United States and that the success of socialistic policies in Europe can provide Americans with a path toward greater prosperity and peace. Such notions are dangerous—not only because socialism has repeatedly been shown to worsen economies and lead to tyranny, but, most importantly, because socialism is an inherently evil system that, despite its adherents' good-hearted intentions, necessitates immoral acts and destroys individual liberty.

1

What Is Socialism?

Perhaps the best argument socialists make about their political beliefs is that few people in the modern Western world understand what socialism is. Although the word is often thrown around in various political debates, both positively and negatively, many people in Europe and the United States don't understand the traditional Marxist view of socialism.

Most of the confusion over socialism is understandable, as I'll explain later in this book, but it has also presented significant challenges *and* opportunities for those who have embraced this ideology. Because people generally don't understand what socialism is, socialists, liberals, and progressives have been able to sway many people into identifying as "socialist" despite having very little in common with the historical ideas associated with this political philosophy.

When Westerners think of socialism, even self-described socialists, they typically imagine specific socialized industries or authoritarian regimes, but rarely do they contemplate the socialized
societies Marx and others dreamed of making. For instance, many
American socialists support single-payer health care, free college
tuition, and other progressive policy ideas, but very few of these
people openly advocate for the socialization of agriculture or requiring all industries to be collectively owned.

The primary challenge many socialists face resulting from people's lack of understanding about socialism is that they constantly
feel like they must defend their views against what socialists consider to be caricatures of their system. For example, it's become
quite common for American libertarians and conservatives to refer
to the collapsing Venezuelan economy as a prime example of how
socialism fails, even though Venezuela hasn't completely adopted
many Marxist ideas.

One of the reasons few people understand what socialism would
look like in its fully developed form is both conservatives and liberals in the United States have used the term as a catch-all for policies
that increase the power of the government, especially the national
government. This is, to some extent, a fair use of the word. A "socialized" medical system is one in which the government pays for
and/or operates the delivery of all health care services—or at least
pays for all health care services. Such a system is socialistic in that

it emphasizes and empowers the collective over the rights of the individual citizen and business owner, but it's a far cry from the socialism of Karl Marx and Friedrich Engels, two of the most influential socialists in history.

Before I outline the essential components of Marx's socialism, it's important to remember that although Marx's ideas have been more influential than the ideas of any other socialist, socialism, similar to other economic and political systems, is a big-tent ideology that includes numerous ideas and philosophies. Just like there is no clear definition of "conservative" or "liberal," with socialism, you'll find many politicians, pundits, and parties with very different policy proposals and political philosophies.

In this book, I've chosen to focus on Marx's socialism, which in its final stage is called "communism," and the "European-style socialism," sometimes referred to as "democratic socialism," found throughout Western Europe, Canada, and the United States. These two brands of socialism pose the greatest threats for capitalists in the West and are the most likely to become more popular over the next century.

The following sections describe socialism as Marx and his ideological descendants understood it, followed by a brief description of how these ideas differ with the more moderate European-style socialism, which may not rise to the level of being considered "evil" but certainly shares many of the same moral issues found in Marx's socialism.

Class Warfare

Central to every Marxist socialist system is the elimination of so-cietal "classes," which virtually all socialists say are to blame for the alleged "exploitation" they believe naturally results from there being separate economic groups in society with varying degrees of wealth. Simply defined, classes are merely groups with different amounts of wealth, and thus different degrees of economic "pow-er." They are often written and spoken about by socialists in broad terms, but logically, in any society in which there are two or more groups with varying amounts of wealth, those groups could reason-ably be called "classes."

Marx spent a substantial amount of his *Communist Manifesto*, his most famous work, describing the history of class warfare and the exploitation of the "working class." But perhaps his most fa-mous passage on the topic appears below. (Don't worry if you're confused about how the terms "socialism" and "communism" re-late, communism and socialism are discussed on page 18.):

The history of all hitherto existing societies is the history of class struggles. Freeman and slave, patrician and plebeian, lord and serf, guild-master and journeyman, in a word, oppressor and op-pressed, stood in constant opposition to one another, carried on an uninterrupted, now hidden, now open fight, a fight that each time ended, either in a revolutionary re-constitution of society at large, or in the common ruin of the contending classes. In the earlier epochs of history, we find almost everywhere a complicated arrangement of society into various orders, a manifold gradation of social rank. In ancient Rome we have patricians, knights, plebeians, slaves; in the Middle Ages, feudal lords, vassals, guild-masters, journeymen, apprentices, serfs; in almost all of these classes, again, subordinate gradations.[1]

Socialism, According to Socialists

Marxist socialists attempt to resolve the world's "exploitation" problem by destroying classes entirely. A vital aspect of this effort, as The Socialist Party of Great Britain explains below, is "common ownership" of property:

> Central to the meaning of socialism is common ownership. This means the resources of the world being owned in common by the entire global population.

> But does it really make sense for everybody to own everything in common? Of course, some goods tend to be for personal consumption, rather than to share—clothes, for example. People 'owning' certain personal possessions does not contradict the principle of a society based upon common ownership.

---

1   Karl Marx, *The Communist Manifesto*, Amazon Digital Services, Kindle Edition, n.d., pp. 13–14, ASIN: B00MJJ7YZE.

In practice, common ownership will mean everybody having the right to participate in decisions on how global resources will be used. It means nobody being able to take personal control of resources, beyond their own personal possessions.[2]

Marx advocated strongly for the end of private property throughout his writings, including in *The Communist Manifesto*. According to Marx:

The distinguishing feature of Communism is not the abolition of property generally, but the abolition of bourgeois property. But modern bourgeois private property is the final and most complete expression of the system of producing and appropriating products, that is based on class antagonisms, on the exploitation of the many by the few. In this sense, the theory of the Communists may be summed up in the single sentence: Abolition of private property.[3]

Under many socialist models, in line with Marx's view, all or nearly all property is owned collectively. There are no private businesses. There are few, if any, markets. In fact, many Marxist social-

2   "What Is Socialism?," The Socialist Party of Great Britain, accessed May 25, 2018, https://www.worldsocialism.org/spgb/what-socialism.

3   Karl Marx, *supra* note 1, p. 13.

ists say a truly socialist society would be completely free of money, too. As The Socialist Party of Great Britain notes, socialism "would entail an end to buying, selling and money. Instead, we would take freely what we had communally produced. The old slogan of 'from each according to ability, to each according to needs' would apply."

The Socialist Party USA also emphasizes the importance of common ownership of property. On its website, this socialist organization notes, "In a socialist system the people own and control the means of production and distribution through democratically controlled public agencies, cooperatives, or other collective groups. The primary goal of economic activity is to provide the necessities of life, including food, shelter, health care, education, child care, cultural opportunities, and social services."[4]

In a world with few, if any, markets and perhaps no money, people would get the products and services they need from the collective (many socialists would reject that this group should be called a "government") without having to "pay" for anything.

How exactly would this scheme work? Socialists have come up with a range of theories, including the use of vouchers. Under a voucher system, instead of buying groceries each week with money, you would present a clerk with a grocery voucher entitling you to a predetermined amount of food products for you and your family.

---

4   Note that not all socialists agree that there shouldn't be markets. Some believe markets can operate within a socialist model, but only if all the means of production (all industry) is collectively owned.

The same would be true for virtually all other goods and services, including clothing, consumer electronics, and housing. People would get what they "need," but not necessarily what they want, and there would be protections in place to keep some people from taking more than others in society or from "exploiting" others through the accumulation of wealth.

The Will of the People

A key feature of virtually every modern socialist movement is its commitment to democracy. For those of you who, like myself, spend a substantial amount of time listening to or reading conservative thinkers, you might be surprised to hear of the important role democracy plays in modern socialist thought, but there's no question whatsoever that for many socialists, a fully formed socialist system must be controlled democratically. This isn't to say that there haven't been people who sought to create collectivist societies using authoritarian means; the history of Marxism is full of such people. However, in modern socialism, very few are calling for authoritarian control of the means of production, and Marx's view of how socialism ought to work precluded any notion of a ruling class governing the rest of society.

The Socialist Party of Great Britain explains, "Democratic control is ... essential to the meaning of socialism. Socialism will be a society in which everybody will have the right to participate in the social decisions that affect them. These decisions could be on a wide range of issues—one of the most important kinds of decision, for example, would be how to organise the production of goods and services."[5]

The Socialist Party USA claims, "Socialism and democracy are one and indivisible," and defines democratic socialism as "a political and economic system with freedom and equality for all, so that people may develop to their fullest potential in harmony with others."[6]

The Democratic Socialists of America say "the essence of the socialist vision" is "that people can freely and democratically control their community and society …" This notion is "central to the movement for radical democracy."[7]

World Government

One of the most important and often overlooked aspects of socialism is that according to many of its proponents, in socialism's purest form, the inhabitants of the world—not individual countries, towns, or cities—would share their resources equally and collectively make decisions. There would be no national borders, as we define them

---

5   The Socialist Party of Great Britain, *supra* note 2.

6   "Socialism As Radical Democracy: Statement of Principles of the Socialist Party USA," Socialist Party USA, accessed May 25, 2018, https://www.socialistpartyusa.net/principles-points-of-agreement.

7   "Where We Stand: Building the Next Left," Democratic Socialists of America, accessed May 25, 2018, http://www.dsausa.org/where_we_stand#dc.

today, no national banks or currencies, and no national armies.

In The Socialist Party of Great Britain's "Object and Declaration of Principles," which were established by the party in 1904, socialism's global character is emphasized:

The world is a "global village." Each region may have its own particular and distinct customs, but they are part of a greater system of society that is world-wide. This system of society is capitalism and every region and nation operates within this system of society in one way or another. Socialism is not a cooperative island in the middle of capitalism, but a global system of society that will replace capitalism.[8]

Marx explained that in his socialist-communist model, countries and nationalities wouldn't necessarily disappear, but that the "exploitation" of one nation by another would evaporate, suggesting the global sharing of resources:

The Communists are further reproached with desiring to abolish countries and nationality.

The working men have no country. We cannot take from them

---

8   "Our Object and Declaration of Principles," The Socialist Party of Great Britain, originally published in 1904, accessed May 25, 2018, https://www.worldsocialism.org/spgb/our-object-and-declaration-principles.

what they have not got. Since the proletariat[9] must first of all acquire political supremacy, must rise to be the leading class of the nation, must constitute itself the nation, it is, so far, itself national, though not in the bourgeois[10] sense of the word.

National differences and antagonisms between peoples are daily more and more vanishing, owing to the development of the bourgeoisie, to freedom of commerce, to the world-market, to uniformity in the mode of production and in the conditions of life corresponding thereto.

The supremacy of the proletariat will cause them to vanish still faster. United action, of the leading civilised countries at least, is one of the first conditions for the emancipation of the proletariat. In proportion as the exploitation of one individual by another is put an end to, the exploitation of one nation by another will also be put an end to.

---

9 In Marx's writings, the "proletariat" is essentially the global "working class" in society—those who produce the world's food, buildings, machinery, etc. with their labor.

10 In Marx's writings, the "bourgeois" is the economic ruling class in society—those who control most of the world's capital. It's better not to think of these individuals as royalty or even as the world's wealthiest people, but rather as the relatively large group, although still much smaller than the working class, in society that controls the overwhelming majority of the industries.

In proportion as the antagonism between classes within the nation vanishes, the hostility of one nation to another will come to an end.[11]

It's also worth mentioning here that although numerous socialist parties focus exclusively on national reforms, for socialism to work *anywhere* effectively, it must be working *everywhere*. As it was explained at the beginning of this chapter, socialism and communism are primarily focused on resolving problems that their adherents believe exist due to the existence of classes. Without classes, they argue, most of the world's crises could be solved through the equitable sharing of resources.

Without a global socialist system, it would likely be impossible to have a classless society, and thus inconceivable a pure socialist system could ever be fully implemented. Although it's theoretically possible to have separate nations with equal amounts of wealth, talent, capital, people, natural resources, etc., in reality, this never occurs. This means class differences in a world without a global socialist structure are unavoidable because variations between nations—even socialist nations—would, in effect, create separate classes.

The Road to a Socialist Utopia

Socialists disagree as to whether a socialist system could be implemented immediately or gradually, with the socialist consensus

---

11   Karl Marx, *supra* note 1, pp. 18–19.

changing over time. Today, many socialist parties and activists suggest the world's globalized economy makes the prospect of a near-immediate implementation more likely than in the nineteenth century, when the ideas of Marx, Engels, and other socialists gained significant popularity.

In Marx's *The Communist Manifesto*, Marx outlined 10 steps the "most advanced" nations could take to move closer to a classless society. According to Marx, these nations would experience/institute:

1. Abolition of property in land and application of all rents of land to public purposes.
2. A heavy progressive or graduated income tax.
3. Abolition of all right of inheritance.
4. Confiscation of the property of all emigrants and rebels.
5. Centralisation of credit in the hands of the State, by means of a national bank with State capital and an exclusive monopoly.
6. Centralisation of the means of communication and transport in the hands of the State.
7. Extension of factories and instruments of production owned by the State; the bringing into cultivation of waste-lands, and the improvement of the soil generally in accordance with a common plan.
8. Equal liability of all to labour. Establishment of industrial armies, especially for agriculture.
9. Combination of agriculture with manufacturing industries;

gradual abolition of the distinction between town and country, by a more equable distribution of the population over the country. 10. Free education for all children in public schools. Abolition of children's factory labour in its present form.[12]

Regardless of the specific steps taken to transition to a fully formed socialist model and the length of time required to make such a transition, one thing is clear, according to Marx: "the first step in the revolution by the working class, is to raise the proletariat to the position of ruling as to win the battle of democracy."

What About Communism?

One of the most significant signs displaying how little the public in the West knows about socialism is in its lack of understanding of how socialism and communism relate.

Throughout the course of this chapter, I've used much material from Marx's *The Communist Manifesto* alongside official materials issued by modern socialist parties to help explain the defining features of socialism. One of the reasons I chose to do this—other than because of Marx's importance and influence—is because there are few, if any, differences between the purest and most complete forms of socialism and what Marx called "communism." In the nineteenth century, many writers used "socialism" and "communism" interchangeably, and in numerous cases, socialist writers relied on oth-

---

12   *Ibid.*, pp. 20–21.

er terms to describe their imagined utopia, including "co-operative commonwealth" and "social republic."[13]

Socialist Adam Buick, writing for the *Socialist Standard*, outlines the long history of the two terms and how they have both been distorted to mean something other than what the leading socialist thinkers intended when they used them in the nineteenth century. Buick notes in his article that the term "socialism" was eventually corrupted and commonly used to "describe measures taken by the State to try to aid the poor":

"State socialism," again, was a term used to describe measures taken by the State to try to aid the poor. The word socialism unfortunately in widespread usage has never lost its association with reforms and reformism. Hence Labour and similar parties in other parts of the world describe themselves and are described as "socialist." This does not deter us from insisting that our use, to describe someone who works for a new society based on common ownership and democratic control of the means of production, is not only the more adequate definition but also the more historically justified: those who introduced the word into English, the Owenites, favoured a co-operative commonwealth

---

13   Adam Buick, "A Question of Definition: (4) Socialism/ Communism," *Socialist Standard*, Issue 886, June 1978, https:// www.worldsocialism.org/spgb/socialist-standard/1970s/1978/no-886-june-1978/question-definition-4-socialismcommunism.

rather than reform of capitalism.[14]

Buick notes the term communism "has suffered a fate just as bad, if not worse."[15]

If Buick's assessment is accurate, why are there so many writers, politicians, and pundits who seem convinced Marx's socialism and communism are two distinct political systems?

For instance, in a *Daily Dot* article titled "What is Socialism, Really?"—a piece that is rather favorable to self-described "democratic socialist" Sen. Bernie Sanders (I-VT)—writer David Gilmour argues socialism and communism are not the same, even though "Marx's writing was a school of far-left socialist thought ..."

Gilmour wrote, "Communism required the state own and manage the distribution of wealth and property according to need."

"Socialism," Gilmour added, "is a more moderate—yet still radical—economic philosophy that seeks to empower the worker through co-ownership of industrial and production capacity and through consensus, whether governmental mechanism or through smaller syndicates."[16]

Gilmour's view, while commonly espoused, is in complete con-

---

14   *Ibid.*

15   *Ibid.*

16   David Gilmour, "What Is Socialism, Really?," *The Daily Dot*, June 28, 2017, https://www.dailydot.com/layer8/what-is-socialism-definition/.

tradition to much of the socialist-communist material I've read from socialist and communist parties and nineteenth century writers. Marx and other early "communists" stated quite often that in their utopian societies, there would *not* be a modern "state" to own and control how property should be used. The existence of a "state"—at least in the sense that Gilmour suggests— necessitates the presence of a separate class, which completely violates Marx's socialist-communist thinking.

Buick, writing on behalf of The Socialist Party of Great Britain, adamantly declared, "As far as we are concerned, socialism and communism are exact synonyms, alternative names to describe the future society we wish to see established and defined in our Object."[17]

If socialism and communism are very similar or even the same, why then do so many people like Gilmour believe they are completely different?

Buick explains in his article that critics who claim communism is some sort of a final, perfected form of socialism are "quite wrong" and that this notion "dates from after 1917 and was an innovation introduced by [Vladimir] Lenin.":

Lenin's innovation (to use a neutral term) was to make "socialism" and "communism" thus defined successive societies after the abolition of capitalism and to attribute this view to Marx (a gross

---

17   Adam Buick, *supra* note 13.

distortion since Marx made no such distinction: he only distin-
guished a "first phase" of "communist society" when there would
still have to be some restrictions on individual consumption—a
reasonable assumption for 1875 but outdated today—from a
"higher phase" when the principle "from each according to his
abilities, to each according to his needs" would apply, but these
were phases of the same society based on common ownership and
democratic control and not successive, separate societies).[18]

Why would Lenin do this? According to Buick, the alteration
was deliberate: "This goes back to a decision of the Bolsheviks in
1918 to change the name of their party from Social Democratic to
Communist Party. They did this to distinguish themselves from the
Social Democratic parties of the rest of Europe which had so shame-
fully betrayed the working class over the war. From then on communist has been used to describe supporters of Russia, inaccurately
... "[19]

European-Style 'Socialism'

Much ground has been covered over the course of this chapter, but
I think it's fair to say Marx's socialism should be defined as a classless, mostly stateless, democratic economic and political system under which all or nearly all private property ownership, especially

---

18   *Ibid.*

19   *Ibid.*

the "means of production," is abolished and replaced by a system in which property is owned collectively. Further, in Marx's system, society embraces the general operating principle "from each according to ability, to each according to needs."

At this point, you may be wondering where modern "European-style socialism," also commonly referred to in America as "democratic socialism," fits into our discussion of socialism. If you've been paying attention, then you already know what many modern European "socialists" call "socialism" isn't Marx's socialism at all; it's a quasi-market system that uses state control, manipulation, and welfare programs to socialize—for the lack of a better word—particular *industries* in society.

For instance, many developed nations have socialized medical systems or socialized health insurance industries, where the government runs and/or pays for health care. Government-dominated health care systems can fairly be called "socialized" because the whole of society participates in the system, and taxpayers are forced to contribute to it.

However, the presence of socialized industries does not make a nation "socialist" in the historical, Marxist sense. Neither does calling oneself "socialist" or "communist." China is a "communist" country, but the truth is the modern Chinese system is quite far from imitating Marx's classless, worker-dominated model.

Conclusion

Before continuing, it's worth acknowledging there are numerous other views of socialism that have been espoused by philosophers, political parties, and activists throughout the history of the nineteenth, twentieth, and twenty-first centuries. In many cases, these ideologies present the same ideas as those discussed above but propose different ways of implementing Marx's dream of a classless society. In other cases, socialists are more concerned with achieving more-realistic, short-term goals, such as dramatically redistributing wealth through draconian income taxes and socializing specific industries, such as health care or higher education.

In all these forms of socialism, one thing is clear: Socialists' primary aim is to push the world in the direction of there being fewer classes, less wealth disparity, and more collectively owned industries and property.

In Chapter Three of this book, I outline the reasons why I believe Marx's socialism is an inherently immoral system. Because so much of the current debate focuses on European-style mixed-socialism (or, according to many Marxists, "mixed-capitalism"), I will critique in this book Marx's socialist utopian society—the same political system supported by many modern Western socialist and communist parties—as well as the European-style mixed-socialist economic system. It is my contention that both models, while very different, are immoral systems that greatly hinder individual freedom, although European-style socialism does not rise to the same level of immorality as Marx's socialism.

Before evaluating the morality of such models, however, I will address in Chapter Two whether Marx's vision for the world is possible to achieve—a consideration that will prove important when we consider the practical effects that result when communities attempt to pursue Marx's socialism.

2

Is Socialism Possible?

In Chapter One, I explained what socialism entails—both the communist version advanced by Karl Marx and the modern European-style socialism of Sweden and other Western European countries. In this short chapter, I'll examine whether Marx's popular view of socialism is practical—or even possible.

Before doing so, it's important to note that Marxist socialists are often the first to point out Marx's vision for a classless society has never been fully implemented anywhere in the history of the world. In fact, it's common for modern socialists to allege that the very same examples of failed socialism so often presented by those of us who support individual liberty are really nothing more than bastardized forms of capitalism. Cambodia, China, the Soviet Union, Venezuela—these are, at least in the minds of some modern socialists—absolutely *not* examples of Marxist socialism.

You might be surprised to hear that on this point, I agree with proponents of socialism; any socialist society in which there are distinct classes, oppressive regimes, and state-sponsored violence cannot be examples of what Marx dreamed of achieving.

With that said, I disagree completely with the belief that Marxism is possible to fully implement—not only today, but at any point in the future, too. My primary reason for believing this is the case is because key aspects of Marx's socialism are totally incompatible with essential features of human nature. It is my view that there has never been a truly socialist state for the same reason there has never been a flying pig or a four-sided triangle: it's completely impossible.

Socialism's Fatal Flaw

Marxist socialists have built their entire system on several deeply flawed assumptions, but perhaps the most critical is in Marx's socialism it is assumed that it is possible to convince virtually everyone to abandon their natural tendency to embrace competition and ambition. Socialists frame competition as the fruit of greedy ruling-class leaders' schemes, not as the result of human nature. According to socialists, we compete because we believe we must, and the reason we believe we must compete is because those who control the means of production have fooled all the peoples of the world into thinking competition is normal.

This view is proven false by virtually every aspect of the human experience. From the time children first begin to interact with one another to the moment we die, all humans experience and embrace some form of competition, even when they don't need to. Young children race each other in school yards. Siblings compete with one another for attention from parents. Children play cards and board games. High schoolers compete with one another in various clubs, classrooms, and for admission to colleges. Hundreds of millions of people, young and old, watch competitive sporting events every year. It is only natural then that humans extend that competitive spirit to the marketplace as well.

Some socialists say humans only compete with one another because they have been indoctrinated to do so. They claim what seems "natural" and "normal" only appears to be so because we're all the victims of immense propaganda campaigns and institutional biases. But socialists ignore competition is evident throughout the natural world. All animals compete for food, resources, territory, and/ or mates, as any biologist will tell you. A competitive spirit isn't instilled into humans because of capitalists' trickery, it's an inherent part of life for all creatures on Earth.

Some socialists might accept that humans are by nature competitive, but they would reject that this competitive spirit must enter the workplace. They insist instead that all economies can properly function without any competition. How, in practice, would this work itself out?

The Lazy Factory Worker

Imagine a fictional nation in which the entire economy is socialized in line with Marx's ideology. Now, imagine Don and Lazy Bill work at an automotive plant, where they each have identical jobs on the plant's assembly line.

Don is an exceptional worker. He works faster and harder than everyone else on the line, including Lazy Bill, who is the plant's least-productive worker. Not only is Don an outstanding employee, he's a pleasure to be around and has exceptional leadership qualities, regularly going above and beyond his position's requirements.

Lazy Bill is not only the plant's worst employee, he's also a poor communicator and unwilling to fulfill his duties in a timely manner. Lazy Bill isn't bad at his job because he's intellectually or physically incapable of doing it, he just doesn't enjoy working as much as Don does.

In Marx's socialist scheme, Don and Lazy Bill would each receive exactly the same amount of wealth to satisfy their "needs"— food, clothing, housing, etc. Even though Don's work is unquestionably more important to the factory, he wouldn't receive any additional benefits.

Some workers—perhaps even our fictional worker Don—might continue to work at a productive pace despite Lazy Bill's performance and the apparent unfairness of a system that provides all workers, regardless of talent or work ethic, the same amount of wealth. Don might enjoy his job so much that he doesn't need any additional incentives to work more efficiently. But what about the rest of the workers in the factory, those who aren't as unproductive as Lazy Bill but also don't enjoy working as much as Don?

In socialism, for a nation's productivity to remain the same, all workers must continue to produce at the same rate without financial incentives as they do with financial incentives, or else the entire economy's productivity inevitably will decline. So, the workers watching Lazy Bill collect the same wealth every week as they do would need to continue working at a high rate out of some altruistic desire for the community, nation, or world, not because it's in their own best interests to do so.

Wherever such a model has been imposed on a large scale, productivity has nearly always fallen absent some other motivation (fear of war, for instance, or violence). The reason is obvious: When the lowest-performing, laziest workers receive the same wealth as the highest-performing, hardest-working individuals, there's little, if any, motivation for most people to work as hard or harder than the most productive employee. Instead, the entire factory workforce only needs to work as hard as the least-productive person. Put simply, the entire socialist economy is a race to the bottom.

The Happiest Sewage Treatment Plant on Earth

Many modern Socialists argue that in their model, workers have the power to choose the jobs they are most passionate about, so, they reason, productivity concerns aren't an issue. In other words, the only people who will work in factories are those who truly desire to. In socialism, everyone gets to do what they love.

If this all sounds too good to be true, it's because this view is totally devoid of economic realities. For any modern society to function properly, there must be, at the very least, essential services—many of which involve jobs virtually no one would take in a world in which all people receive the same wealth for their work.

For instance, in a socialist utopian America, thousands of people would voluntarily work at the nation's sewage treatment plants, where some would be required to spend their days wading through thousands of tons of human excrement in return for the same wealth as the person powdering donuts at Disney World.

Similarly, who's going to work the cleanup crews in slaughterhouses or spend their days clearing trash from America's streets for the same wealth as those who spend five hours per day playing with puppies?

What About Those Who Won't Work?

The most problematic group in a socialist society isn't the nation's unproductive workers; it's those who choose not to work at all. When asked what would happen with these individuals, socialists have provided a wide range of responses. However, historically, the most common reaction by those attempting to build a socialist society has been to use force—prison, violence, threats—to compel people to work or to work more productively.

However, as I previously noted, in a truly socialist society, there are *zero* class differences. There are no ruling government officials or oppressive regimes. In such a scheme, how are those treated who don't want to work in factories or sewage treatment plants, as garbage collectors, or in any other position?

Interestingly, many modern socialists argue these folks need not work at all. According to this theory, there is plenty of wealth to go around without needing all able-bodied people to work, so all those who don't want to work could pursue their own personal interests instead.

Parts of this argument are admittedly difficult to disprove using data. There is no historical precedence for an economic system in which only those who enjoy working are asked to work while everyone else takes a lifelong paid vacation. And it's effectively impossible to calculate how many people in society would choose not to work if given the option. Basic logic suggests, however, that if no one *must* work, most people won't.

What about the argument claiming there's so much global wealth that many people wouldn't need to work if all that wealth were to be redistributed equally? According to a 2017 report by Credit Suisse, there is about $280 trillion of wealth in the world today. That sounds quite impressive, but when you divide that immense amount of wealth out equally among the world's 7.6 billion people, each individual would only receive less than $37,000, or about $57,000 per adult—and that includes the value of land.[20,21]

As numerous others have noted, including Don Watkins and Yaron Brook in their book *Equal Is Unfair: America's Misguided Fight Against Income Inequality*, the only way to have true equality today would be for all people to live in miserable poverty. And that problem would be made much worse in a world in which no one is required, either through market forces or by some other means, to work.

The Impossible Dream

If you were to boil down all of Marxist thinking into one idea, it would be that Marx wanted to end classes—which simply means he did not want there to be varying degrees of wealth. According to Marx, everyone should get what they need—not necessarily what they want—and no one should have noticeably more wealth than anyone else. Society would be classless and, in many respects, without any markets (as we understand them today).

Even if we could have a nation or world in which all people voluntarily shared all wealth equally, there are several severe problems that undercut much of Marx's thinking. For instance, in a world

---

20   Robert Frank, "Richest 1% now owns half the world's wealth," CNBC.com, November 14, 2017, https://www.cnbc.com/2017/11/14/richest-1-percent-now-own-half-the-worlds-wealth.html.

21   *Global Wealth Report 2017*, Credit Suisse Research, 2017, http://publications.credit-suisse.com/tasks/render/file/index.cfm?fileid=12DFFD63-07D1-EC63-A3D5F67356880EF3.

without classes, how would finite resources like land be distributed?

Malibu or Topeka?

There's nothing wrong with Topeka, Kansas, but given the choice (assuming there is no such thing as wealth disparity or money), it's safe to say far more people would choose to live in Malibu, California than in Topeka. But in a socialist model, where there are no classes, how could the tens of millions of people in America who want to live in Malibu have the ability to do so? It's certainly possible *thousands* of people could move to the Malibu region if all the land in the area were to be confiscated, but there simply isn't enough space for everyone to live in Malibu who wants to.

This might sound like a ridiculous problem, but it illustrates the foolishness of the socialist model. Even if all people were to have the same house, yard, etc., not everyone would get to live in Malibu, which means, in effect, you would have "classes" of people—those who get to live in Malibu and those who want to but can't.

There are significant economic considerations to keep in mind as well. Even if you could find enough gorgeous lands throughout the United States to satisfy everyone today, what happens in 500 years, when there are hundreds of millions of additional Americans? How can everyone live in the places they want to in an increasingly populated world?

Even more importantly, not everyone can live in their ideal locations, because if they did, there likely wouldn't be enough people to work America's massive farmlands, cut down trees, drill for oil and natural gas, etc. Not everyone can live in their paradise, because paradise is often not located where important natural resources and industries are situated.

To these objections, socialists insist enough people would choose voluntarily to live and work throughout the country, including in those regions where most of America's food is grown and energy is gathered and distributed. But that assessment is based on absolutely no evidence. What is clear, though, is that a group of people working on a farm in northern Minnesota would have a very different life than those who don't work at all and have homes located on Malibu's beaches—and "different," at least to some people, would surely feel a lot like the creation of classes.

Another concern related to land is the role property rights play in ensuring lands are taken care of. In many socialist models, property would be redistributed when a person occupying that land dies. This is, in my opinion, an essential feature of Marxist property ownership, because if land can continually be passed down, more-desirable lands would never be given away by families, effectively creating a hereditary class. But if land ownership is always temporary, then what incentive is there to improve upon it, protect it, or use it efficiently? None, of course. In fact, any efforts made for these purposes would be extremely inefficient, because individuals and their families would be able to gain nothing from them in a cashless, marketless society that doesn't permit families to pass down property.

A Delusional Utopia

There's much more that could be said about why Marx's socialism appears to be nothing more than a wild fiction, but there are many more important moral concerns that now need to be considered, which I'll do in the next chapter.

What I hope has been clear by this point, however, is that the common thread that runs through all of Marx's thinking, as well as the thinking of many modern socialists, is that property ownership should be collective and that Marxists believe their system will work because people will *choose* to behave in ways that seem contradictory to all of human history and nature.

In Marxism, future humans will not be nearly as concerned about competition or their own personal welfare as they are today. They will voluntarily choose to work the jobs no one wants, and they will do so in exchange for the exact same wealth everyone else receives. Future laborers will also agree to work even while knowing they receive no additional wealth or benefits as a result of that labor and while knowing that if they were to choose to stop working, they could pursue their own hobbies and personal interests whenever they want. Additionally, these people would voluntarily elect to manage their property efficiently and effectively knowing they and their family will never benefit from that additional work.

These ideas aren't only radical, they are delusional. But it's important to remember there's nothing inherently *evil* about advocating for a system that very likely won't work. To prove my primary claim—that socialism is dangerously immoral, to the point of being classified as "evil"—several important ideas must be discussed at length, which I'll now do in Chapter Three.

3

Socialism Is Evil

Winston Churchill, one of the twentieth century's most important and influential leaders, once said in a speech before the United Kingdom's House of Commons, "The inherent vice of capitalism is the unequal sharing of blessings. The inherent virtue of socialism is the equal sharing of miseries."

Since Churchill delivered these remarks, little has changed in the way supporters of individual freedom address socialism; generally speaking, the emphasis is always placed on why socialism isn't an effective economic system.

In Chapter Two of this book, I spent a little bit of time outlining some of the reasons I believe Marx's view of socialism, the same philosophy espoused by many of the world's modern socialist parties, is severely flawed. However, the primary purpose of this book isn't to present an open-and-shut case against the effectiveness of socialism. Why? Because although it's true that whenever Marx's socialism has been attempted (it's never been fully implemented), it has always ended in tragedy, American progressives, socialists, and other leftists have been quite successful in convincing millions of people to believe socialism can work and that the mixed-market socialized societies of Europe are models that should be adopted everywhere, including in the United States.

Too often, the debate focuses on results rather than morals, and it's easy for the Left to manipulate results, make false promises, or cherry-pick data to "prove" that socialist systems can and do work. And whenever a crafty leftist finds himself or herself backed into a corner in a policy debate, he or she simply reverts to the old, albeit effective, argument alleging, "If we had higher taxes, all of our policies would work."

Further, it's difficult to disprove hypotheticals, so the fact that socialism in its purest form has never been implemented creates significant challenges for opponents of communism and socialism, especially because socialists' promises of a utopian society in which all people everywhere have everything they need is so alluring. Who doesn't want to live in a country where there is no poverty, violence, or ruling classes? Who doesn't want to live in a world where everyone has health coverage, access to college, and guaranteed wealth?

Many young people are especially susceptible to such promises. Millennials such as myself didn't live through the fall of the Soviet

Union, the reeducation camps of Mao's communist China, or the Cambodian killing fields. When they think of socialistic policies, they think of Scandinavia, not Nazi Germany.

To win the ideological war against socialism, the debate needs to focus on the numerous moral problems with socialism, not whether socialist systems are effective at providing food, shelter, education, or health care. The reason I believe this is *not* because I think it's impossible to argue free markets are more effective at making societies happier and healthier; history has proven over and over that liberty does lead to greater prosperity. This argument is more difficult to make, however, because it requires people to have a deep knowledge of history, current events, and political philosophy—an important caveat in an America in which leftists control virtually every level of the education system, most of the country's primary media outlets, Hollywood, and most of the music industry.

Further, by fixating on complex economic, social, and cultural problems associated with socialism, supporters of liberty have abandoned the moral high ground, which is why they routinely find themselves arguing socialism is a nice utopian thought but isn't realistic, rather than arguing socialism is a horrendous, tyrannical ideology, even if it can be proven to be effective at controlling and manipulating every aspect of a nation's economy.

Throughout the remainder of this chapter and in Chapter Four, I'll explore the many moral problems with socialism—both Marxist socialism and the more moderate European-style socialism commonly found in many parts of the world today, including in the United States. I will mostly—although not completely—avoid discussing failed socialist-leaning states and evaluating whether socialist systems are effective at improving people's living standards.

But before explaining why I believe Marx's socialism is evil, I will below briefly define what I mean by "evil" and explain why this term is appropriate for this important discussion.

What Is Evil?

Over the course of human history, "evil" has been used in a variety of ways. In Western Civilization, evil has for nearly 2,000 years been understood within the context of Judeo-Christianity, and a great emphasis has been placed on understanding evil as that which is contrary to the will of God as it has been revealed in scripture. Anything that violates God's law has been considered evil.

In other parts of the world, evil has been defined in a variety of other ways, often shaped by that region's religious beliefs. In countries in which Islam is the primary religion, for instance, evil is typically understood within the framework of the teachings in the Quran.

At the beginning of the nineteenth century, these views began to fade with the rise of secularism and various anti-religious movements in the West. Of course, religious people maintain their religion-specific understanding of "evil," but throughout most of Western society, including in America, "evil" has effectively come to mean "morally reprehensible" and that which arises "from actual or imputed bad character or conduct," as the Merriam-Webster dictionary notes.

In a country in which most people don't hold fast to a specific religious set of beliefs, it's difficult to nail down exactly what it means to be "morally reprehensible." This is because, as many American Christian authors have noted in recent years, most people today have no *objective* moral standard by which all actions can be judged.

An objective moral standard is a clear standard of conduct that is considered to be absolutely true. Today, most of the non-Christian, non-Jewish, non-Islamic West has rejected the idea of an objective moral standard, favoring instead the post-modern subjective standard, which is really just another way of saying that morality ought to be determined by each and every person. Only when people collectively agree that a particular behavior, such as murder, for instance, is immoral, can that behavior be rightly considered by the whole of society to be "evil."

While substantially more could be said about evil and morality, for the purposes of this book, all that needs to be agreed upon is that it's immoral to force—using the threat of violence or imprisonment—peaceful people to participate in activities they are morally opposed to. Or, put another way, it's highly immoral to force people to engage in actions they believe are immoral.

For instance, I think the overwhelming majority of Americans would agree it would be highly immoral for the government to force a gay couple to give their money to groups that openly call for all gay people to go to prison. Similarly, few, if any, would argue it's incorrect to say it would be immoral to compel with threats of violence or imprisonment a vegetarian to slaughter animals. Most people, including those who support the continued legalization of abortion, would also agree it's evil to *force* women to have abortions.

At the heart of all these issues is a recognition individuals have a natural right to live peacefully without having to violate their conscience. By "natural right," I mean every single person is born with this right. No one, including government, gives it to you. Simply by existing, you have the right to live without being compelled by force to violate your conscience. This is why in America we don't force pacifists to kill people on foreign battlefields or imprison doctors who don't want to perform abortions.

This, of course, doesn't mean people can do anything they want. Individual freedom is limited to those behaviors and beliefs that don't *directly* harm other people. For instance, a person can't steal from another person and then claim his or her religion permits thievery and thus allows him or her to take others' property whenever that person desires to do so.

In short, it is my firm contention that it is highly immoral to compel people to violate their deeply held and sincere beliefs by forcing them—using the rule of law—to participate in acts they deem to be extremely immoral. A "free society" cannot properly be considered "free" if its citizens do not even have the basic right to abstain from activities they believe to be morally wrong. If people can be forced to engage in immoral actions, then "personal liberty" only exists to the extent the majority of people in society permit it to, which is to say that fundamental human rights don't exist at all.

Collective Property Ownership

As I mentioned in Chapters One and Two, one of the core elements of all Marxist socialist models is the collective ownership of property. In Marx's socialism, most forms of private property are collectively owned. There might be some private personal possessions, but all the so-called "means of production" are owned by the entire community, whether that be a single nation or the entire globe.

Because most or all property is owned collectively in Marxism, all decisions must be made on the behalf of the collective. This is an important aspect of democratic socialism for many of its adherents because if different property-owning groups exist, you can't have a classless society. You could theoretically divide property ownership equally among groups, but those groups would eventually manage their property differently, resulting in some groups having more or better property than others. In Marx's socialism, this can't be permitted, because, again, this would mean a class system would exist or soon develop.

Many democratic socialists argue in the most developed form of Marxism, a society would not include any money and few, if any, markets precisely because people would manage property differently and class systems would eventually emerge. Thus, all or most property must be owned collectively.

There are primarily two ways to go about managing property collectively. The first is to have a small group of people have complete control over the management of property for the whole of society. This model has been embraced by tyrannical governments all over the world and throughout human history. It effectively leads to there being at least two classes in society (and usually more develop): those who control property and those who must live in accordance with whatever those in charge want. North Korea essentially operates this way today.

Many modern Marxists would reject this model and say it violates several fundamental aspects of Marx's socialist thinking. Instead, they advocate for the democratic control of property.

In practice, democratic control of property means the people, through democratic elections, would decide how all property must be used. This could be accomplished either through direct democracy, where every person in society votes for how property should or shouldn't be used, or through a representative democracy, also called a representative republic. Under the representative democracy model, people would elect others to manage property, but the public would continue to maintain control over those they elect.

Because the vast majority of existing socialist parties, groups, and activists in the modern era are calling for a democratic form of socialism, rather than some fascist model, I'll refrain from commenting on other forms of governance. Nearly everyone, including most modern Western socialists, would agree tyrannical forms of government are evil, so there's no point in spilling additional ink arguing against the merits of a system nearly all corners of the Western world rejects.

Hindus or Hamburgers?

In a Marxist democratic socialist model, all decisions would be, directly or indirectly, made collectively and with the whole populace in mind. Each person would own an equal share of all the wealth in that society, so collective decision-making is virtually a necessity.

Marx's idea was that if all property is owned collectively and managed for the good of everyone, then the trillions of dollars of wealth (in modern terms) controlled by corporations, wealthy people, and other members of Marx's "bourgeoisie"—those who control the world's capital—could be used more effectively and to the benefit of working-class people. This means, by definition, all or nearly all economic decisions would be made by the majority of people in society. This is extremely problematic in a society in which people have different moral values, because those with the minority view must inevitably participate in activities they are morally opposed to, including many activities that would violate religious beliefs.

For instance, many Hindus believe killing and eating animals is extremely immoral.[22] In a socialist society, the agricultural indus-

---

22   Wendy Doniger, "Hinduism and its complicated history with

try, like all industries, would be collectively owned and managed. If the majority of people in society votes, either directly or indirectly, to kill cows to produce beef products for consumption, all Hindus in that society must participate. They would, directly or indirectly, support the killing of cows through their labor, and because the cows and virtually all elements of the cow-killing industry would be owned collectively, there would be no way for Hindus to separate themselves from these actions. The society would be forced to choose between violating the religious beliefs of some Hindus or banning hamburgers. There would be no middle ground, because all industries would be owned collectively.

A related problem would exist for those Muslims who might feel uncomfortable contributing to the consumption of pigs, which is a violation of their religion: "Forbidden to you are: dead meat, blood, the flesh of swine, and that on which hath been invoked the name of other than Allah."[23,24]

The same might be true for some Jews, who believe, in accordance with their scriptures, they are not permitted to eat pork: "And the pig, though it has a divided hoof, does not chew the cud; it is un-

---

cows (and people who eat them)," *The Conversation*, July 16, 2017, http://theconversation.com/hinduism-and-its-complicated-history-with-cows-and-people-who-eat-them-80586.

23   See Quran 5:3.

24   "Why do Muslims abstain from pork?," WhyIslam.org, August 9, 2011, https://www.whyislam.org/faqs/restrictions-in-islam/why-do-muslims-abstain-from-pork.

clean for you. You must not eat their meat or touch their carcasses; they are unclean for you."[25]

These concerns don't only apply to those with religious beliefs, either. People for the Ethical Treatment of Animals (PETA), an organization that boasts more than 6.5 million members, states on its website, "Animals are not ours to eat, wear, experiment on, use for entertainment, or abuse in any other way."[26]

In one section of PETA's website, it goes so far as to say animals have "a right to live free from pain and suffering":

Supporters of animal rights believe that animals have an inherent worth—a value completely separate from their usefulness to humans. We believe that every creature with a will to live has a right to live free from pain and suffering. Animal rights is not just a philosophy—it is a social movement that challenges society's traditional view that all nonhuman animals exist solely for human use. As PETA founder Ingrid Newkirk has said, "When it comes to pain, love, joy, loneliness, and fear, a rat is a pig is a dog is a boy. Each one values his or her life and fights the knife."

In a country or world with a socialized agricultural system, it's

25   Book of Leviticus 11:7–8, New International Version of the Bible.

26   "Why Animal Rights?," People for the Ethical Treatment of Animals, accessed June 5, 2018, https://www.peta.org/about-peta/why-peta/why-animal-rights.

highly unlikely animals wouldn't be harmed, especially in Western countries. That means all of PETA's 6.5 million members would be forced to contribute to industries they find reprehensible.

The only way to avoid these and many other similar moral problems would be to ban the killing of animals, which, of course, would mean hundreds of millions of people in the West would be barred from hunting and eating in ways they now enjoy. It would also create a tremendous strain on agriculture and other food providers, because they aren't equipped to handle the massive increase in demand that would be necessary to keep the West from starving or suffering from malnourishment in a world in which animals cannot be killed.

Nuns or Feminists?

The food industry is only one concern, and certainly not the most controversial. While a detailed discussion of contraception is beyond the scope of this book, one thing is beyond any doubt: Some people throughout the world believe contraception is evil while others believe all women have a *right* to have access to contraception.

In the Roman Catholic Church, the official dogmatic teaching of the church is that it is a grave sin, and thus an evil act contrary to God's will, to have sexual relations while using birth control methods that attempt to block conception. On the opposing side of the issue, many feminist groups believe women have a right to have access to various birth control methods, all or nearly of which would be considered in opposition to the Roman Catholic Church's teachings.

In a fully socialized medical system, contraception is either permitted, produced, and provided or it's forbidden. There is no middle ground because there is only one health care provider: the collective. That means either nuns or feminists would be forced to violate their beliefs and participate in a system they oppose.

Gambling

According to a 2013 study of moral attitudes by the Pew Research Center, 24 percent of Americans say they believe gambling is "morally unacceptable." While this group is clearly a minority in the United States, where gambling is widespread, there remains tens of millions of people who believe these activities are morally wrong, and in some cases, those beliefs are linked to religion.[27]

For example, the Church of Jesus Christ of Latter-Day Saints, the largest Mormon church in the world, teaches gambling is morally wrong and should be outlawed: "The Church of Jesus Christ of Latter-day Saints is opposed to gambling, including lotteries sponsored by governments. Church leaders have encouraged Church members to join with others in opposing the legalization and government sponsorship of any form of gambling."[28]

How would gambling activities be treated in a socialist society?

---

27   "Global Views on Morality," Pew Research Center, 2014, accessed June 7, 2018, http://www.pewglobal.org/2014/04/15/global-morality.

28   "Gambling," lds.org, Church of Jesus Christ of Latter-Day Saints, accessed June 7, 2018, https://www.lds.org/topics/gambling?lang=eng.

In socialist-communist society like the one imagined by Karl Marx, there likely would be very limited individual property ownership, making gambling unlikely to occur. But in a society in which many but not all aspects of an economy are socialized, it's conceivable a socialized gambling industry could exist. Indeed, this is precisely what the modern lottery system is: The state operates a gambling operation and uses the proceeds for various government activities.

Although lotteries are mostly or completely paid for by participants, a case can be made those morally opposed to lotteries and other forms of state-sponsored gambling are not currently forced take part in these schemes. This, however, is not completely accurate. Gambling operations don't fall from out of the sky. They must start somewhere, potentially requiring taxpayer funds to get the ball rolling. Further, and more importantly, the funds collected by the lottery are used to pay for numerous government programs, which means most Americans are, whether they realize it or not, in some way benefiting or participating in gambling, including those who believe gambling is immoral.

Alcohol

Mormons and various other religious groups oppose the consumption of alcohol, including some Muslims, Protestant Christian groups, and Seventh-day Adventists. In Pew Research Center's 2013 study of morality, which included respondents from 40 countries, 42 percent of survey participants said "alcohol use" is "morally unacceptable."[29]

In a socialist society in which the economy is completely social-ized, all alcohol distilleries would be collectively owned and oper-ated. Although this wouldn't require anyone to consume alcohol, it would mandate all people participate, either directly or indirectly, in the consumption of alcohol by others. This would violate the con-sciences of those who believe it's immoral to take part in the alcohol industry and force some to violate their religious beliefs.

A Nation of Arms Dealers

In the United States, the Second Amendment in the Bill of Rights protects individuals' right to "bear arms": "A well regulated Militia, being necessary to the security of a free State, the right of the people to keep and bear Arms, shall not be infringed." Although many dis-agree over the exact meaning of this amendment, one thing is clear: American adults have the right to own firearms. (An examination of which firearms and weaponry is beyond the scope of this book.)

The United States is home to some 270 million guns, more guns than anywhere else in the world. Despite the large population of gun owners in America, however, there remains a very large segment of the population that opposes gun ownership for individuals, primari-ly based on the idea guns are too dangerous for most people to own. Even the guns of responsible owners could, they argue, end up in the hands of criminals.

---

29   Pew Research Center, *supra* note 27.

For this reason, and many others, numerous anti-gun advocates say they would never own firearms and don't recommend anyone else own them, either. But in a socialist society in which individuals can own guns, every gun produced must be manufactured by collectively owned gun factories and distributed by collectively owned gun outlets.

As a supporter of the Second Amendment, it is my strong belief private gun ownership is a benefit to society, not a vice. But as an ardent supporter of individual liberty, I think it is incredibly immoral to force people who oppose gun ownership to effectively become part-owners of a weapons factory.

The only way to avoid this problem would be to ban all guns, but this policy is unlikely to work in America for numerous reasons, not the least of which being there are millions of gun owners here who would never peacefully give up their weapons (because they believe they have a natural right to possess them). It's also highly unlikely, no matter how socialized the U.S. economy becomes, an amendment to the Constitution banning gun ownership would ever be ratified by the requisite three-fourths of states. Thus, if America were to adopt socialism, it could likely only do so if all gun manufacturing and distribution were collectively owned.

Cogs in the Wheel

Perhaps no area of life is more personal and important than the relationship between parents and their children. In America, parents have long enjoyed significant protections guaranteeing their right to instill the values in their kids that they believe to be most important. In a socialist system, that would become difficult, if not possible, to achieve.

In Marx's socialism, every part of society, including educational institutions, are run collectively, which means education and professional development are also determined collectively by the majority of voters. Thus, parents' rights only exist to the extent that the majority of people allow them to. And even in societies that permit parents to teach their children whatever they want, the same diversity would be impossible in the government-run school system, where a single organization would ultimately decide what everyone learns at every stage of life. How else could a whole nation or world ensure that there are enough skilled workers in every industry to provide for the needs of the collective?

Some might not be concerned about such an arrangement, especially since many schools and colleges in the West today are funded or run by government. But it's important to remember that in a socialist economy, where all industries are planned and controlled by the collective, there would be a strong incentive for schools to push children into those fields where the collective believes they would be most useful, rather than where their interests are. Children's individual skills and interests would need to make way for the requirements of the rest of society. This means children in a socialist system would become more like cogs in a gigantic wheel than individuals with unique desires and dreams.

Further, who would determine how to teach children about morals, and which morals would be valued? It's certainly possible an educational system could fairly present all of the world's moral systems and allow the children to decide for themselves which ideas to adopt, but there's no guarantee that would occur in a system in which the majority has the power to hire and fire *all* educators and no educational alternatives are permitted. It's much more likely the majority's views, however extreme they might be, would be imposed on the minority through the education system.

This presents some significant moral problems, especially for religious minorities. For instance, in a socialist education model, what can Christian, Jewish, Muslim, and other religious parents do if the school system decides to teach a view of sexual ethics that violates their beliefs? Socialism doesn't allow for diversity because the collective makes decisions for everyone.

Some might suggest that a socialized education system could permit several different kinds of education systems under a larger nationalized or global system, but such a model would violate important aspects of socialist thinking. A truly socialized economy wouldn't permit educational alternatives because such alternatives would mean some people are getting a higher-quality education, which must be outlawed to ensure economic classes do not develop. Socialism can only survive when there are virtually no options. If any options exist, there will inevitably be varying degrees of quality and thus some people will end up with better outcomes than others.

Nowhere to Run: Global Socialism

In Chapter One, I explained some Marxist socialists have reasoned—and correctly so—that regional or even national socialist models cannot work effectively in the long run. They insist that for Marx's socialism to be fully realized, socialism must be adopted on a global scale.

In *The Communist Manifesto*, Marx attempts to refute several criticisms of his socialist ideas, including that it was dangerous that he and others desired "to abolish countries and nationality."[30]

In response, Marx wrote, "The working men have no country. We cannot take from them what they have not got. Since the proletariat must first of all acquire political supremacy, must rise to be the leading class of the nation, must constitute itself the nation, it is, so far, itself national, though not in the bourgeois sense of the word."

Marx later added:

United action, of the leading civilised countries at least, is one of the first conditions for the emancipation of the proletariat. In proportion as the exploitation of one individual by another is put an end to, the exploitation of one nation by another will also be put an end to. In proportion as the antagonism between classes within the nation vanishes, the hostility of one nation to another

---

30   Karl Marx, *supra* note 1, p. 18.

will come to an end.[31]

Marx clearly had a global understanding of socialism in mind, although his writing here doesn't explicitly deny the possibility that there could be separate nations—albeit in a different sense than what is found today. He does suggest, however, that once socialism takes hold worldwide, the "hostility of one nation to another will come to an end," because the exploitation of one nation over another would also end. This only makes sense, if we apply basic logic to Marx's thinking, if socialism is applied worldwide. I say this because Marx repeatedly alleges that the collective control and ownership of property is essential for ending class division, which Marx believed to be one of the root causes of exploitation. If there is no exploitation of one country over another, it must be because there are no classes. And if there are no classes, it must be because there is common property ownership, which would mean national borders would be nonexistent or meaningless.

Friedrich Engels, who worked very closely with Marx, wrote in his *Origin of the Family, Private Property, and the State* that the end of all nation states is unavoidable:

The state, therefore, has not existed from all eternity. There have been societies which have managed without it, which had no notion of the state or state power. At a definite stage of eco-

---

31   *Ibid.*, pp. 18–19.

nomic development, which necessarily involved the cleavage of society into classes, the state became a necessity because of this cleavage. We are now rapidly approaching a stage in the development of production at which the existence of these classes has not only ceased to be a necessity, but becomes a positive hindrance to production. They will fall as inevitably as they once arose. The state inevitably falls with them. The society which organizes production anew on the basis of free and equal association of the producers will put the whole state machinery where it will then belong–into the museum of antiquities, next to the spinning wheel and the bronze ax.

The reason the global nature of socialism is relevant to our discussion about whether socialism is evil is because *all* the concerns mentioned previously about socialism are made significantly worse when applied on a global scale. If people have nowhere on Earth they can go to escape the will of the majority, then the world's minorities must always live in accordance with the demands and standards of the global majority.

For Americans and Europeans, this should be a particularly troubling thought since they are far outnumbered by the rest of the world. In fact, there are likely more people living in Asia than in all other parts of the world combined, which means in a global socialist system, Asia would alone have the power to decide how the world's resources are used.

It must be noted here that this concern is not meant to be an affront on Asian nations or their people. It simply illustrates that in global socialism, economic decision-making would be concentrated in one part of the world, putting at risk the rights of every other part of the world. And while some might say this problem already exists, because nations like the United States have a tremendous amount of power relative to other countries, a global socialist model would create entirely new and much more severe problems, because under a socialist scheme, the majority would, through democratic means, control every piece of collectively owned property.

Marx's Unavoidable and Evil Revolution

In many modern Marxist socialist books and articles, socialists attempt to distance themselves from the failures of numerous self-described "socialist" and "communist" parties, both past and present. This is understandable given the intense criticism socialists often receive by those alleging socialism has already failed horrendously in Cambodia, China, North Korea, the Soviet Union, Venezuela, and elsewhere.

As I've already noted, it's unfair to claim Marx's end goal was a nation dominated by a centralized, oppressive government. Marx's communism specifically prohibited such a ruling class, and modern socialists in the West have made it abundantly clear they support democratic decision-making, not authoritarianism.

However, while Marx's end goal was the decentralization of political and economic power, he did at times acknowledge the need for a working-class revolution during which the working class would temporarily use "force" to seize control of nations and existing authoritative structures. In *The Communist Manifesto*, Marx wrote:

> When, in the course of development, class distinctions have disappeared, and all production has been concentrated in the hands of a vast association of the whole nation, the public power will lose its political character. Political power, properly so called, is merely the organised power of one class for oppressing another. If the proletariat [working class] during its contest with the bourgeoisie [those who control most property] is compelled, by the force of circumstances, to organise itself as a class, if, by means of a revolution, it makes itself the ruling class, and, as such, sweeps away by force the old conditions of production, then it will, along with these conditions, have swept away the conditions for the existence of class antagonisms and of classes generally, and will thereby have abolished its own supremacy as a class.[32]

As Marx makes clear, it may be necessary "by means of a revolution" for the working class to make itself "the ruling class" and "[sweep] away by force the old conditions of production" because doing so will sweep away "the conditions for the existence of class

---

32   Karl Marx, *supra* note 1, p. 21.

antagonisms and classes generally ..."

Many socialist groups and parties are opposed to violent and tyrannical revolutions, but it's not hard to imagine why some who would like to build a utopian socialist society believe the only way to accomplish such a feat would be to forcefully seize political power.

Unless those who control capital, including land, *willingly* give up their property, some kind of tyrannical governmental or revolutionary action is necessary to transition to a world where all or nearly all property is owned collectively. The moral problems associated with such a destruction of private property rights are many and horrifying, but because many modern socialist parties and thinkers deflect such concerns by suggesting most people will choose to willingly give up their property to help usher in the new socialist world, there's no need to address actions that even many socialists acknowledge would be highly immoral. It is worth mentioning here, though, that common sense suggests most people would not give up their property absent some degree of violence; force and coercion are likely necessary to bring socialism into existence.

Conclusion

Marx's vision for a pure socialist-communist world has not yet come to fruition, and it arguably never will because of the many moral and practical problems outlined in previous sections. However, these concerns haven't stopped revolutionaries around the world from attempting to bring about a socialist-communist paradise, and in so doing, killing tens of millions of people and pushing hundreds of millions more into despair.

As I hope I have proven, even if a socialist system could be properly, effectively, and peacefully implemented—something I believe to be an impossibility—the resulting system would sacrifice the rights of the individual and minority groups so that the "collective" could have greater power and control.

To this point, much of this book has focused on the dangers of Marx's socialism, but the greater moral danger in our modern world is very likely the *partial* implementation of Marx's ideas, whereby many nations socialize certain industries without socializing their entire society. In Chapter Four, I'll discuss the significant moral problems related to these "mixed-socialist" systems, many of which are tied closely to the concerns described throughout Chapter Three.

4

European-Style Socialism

Throughout this book, I have referred to mixed economic systems in which several large industries are socialized as "European-style socialism," which is also commonly called "democratic socialism." "European-style socialism" is a term regularly used in America to describe such models, although the truth is all or nearly all the world's developed countries, including the United States, have at least one industry that is heavily socialized. This means that nearly every economy in the developed world is, to one extent or another, "socialistic."

At what point is it accurate to call a country with a mixed-socialist economy "socialist," "European-style socialist," or "democratic socialist" rather than a "mixed-socialist," "mixed-capitalist," or "mixed-market" economy? There is no definitive answer to this question, which means the definition of a "socialist nation" is constantly shifting. Many socialists would say there are no "socialist" nations currently in existence, and if they are referring to Marx's fully formed socialism, they are correct. However, the same argument could be made about capitalism. I'm not aware of a single country that has a truly libertarian free market. Most market economies are heavily regulated and taxed, and many operate alongside large government-run social programs. Thus, one could just as easily reason there's no such thing as a modern "capitalist" nation, either.

Rather than thinking about "socialist nations" versus "capitalist countries," it makes far more sense when evaluating modern European-style socialist nations to consider the morality of specific socialist government programs. Upon doing so, it will become evident that the same moral issues facing Marx's pure communist-socialism plague all modern countries with socialist programs, which for our purposes can be defined as programs whose primary purpose is to socialize an *industry* through collective property ownership.

Collective Health Care

In America, the socialist program not currently in existence that has received the most support from the political Left in recent years—thanks in large part to self-described socialist Sen. Bernie Sanders (D-VT)—is a national single-payer health care program. Although there are many other socialist programs and policies the American political Left would like to implement as well, the problems with socializing health care, which I outline below, are very helpful in understanding how copious moral difficulties can arise from the socialization of a single industry, so I'll spend most of my time in this chapter discussing health care and how morally complex this issue is.

During Sanders' 2016 run for president, he outlined many left-wing policy proposals he pledged to enact if elected president. The proposal that received the most attention was his "Medicare for All" health care plan. According to Sanders' website:

> Bernie's plan would create a federally administered single-payer health care program. Universal single-payer health care means comprehensive coverage for all Americans. Bernie's plan will cover the entire continuum of health care, from inpatient to outpatient care; preventive to emergency care; primary care to specialty care, including long-term and palliative care; vision, hearing and oral health care; mental health and substance abuse services; as well as prescription medications, medical equipment, supplies, diagnostics and treatments. Patients will be able to choose a health care provider without worrying about whether that provider is in-network and will be able to get the care they need without having to read any fine print or trying to figure out how they can afford the out-of-pocket costs.[33]

---

33   "Medicare for All: Leaving No One Behind," berniesanders. com, accessed June 8, 2018, https://live-berniesanders-com.pantheonsite.

In Canada and Europe, there are a variety of single-payer health care models, and Sanders' proposal features many of the same reforms used in those countries. A great deal could be discussed regarding the effectiveness of single-payer programs such as the one proposed by Sanders, but as I have done elsewhere in this book, the primary focus of the brief section below will be the morality of such programs, not their effectiveness.

Sanders' pledge to "cover the entire continuum of health care," while appealing to many, would undoubtedly create numerous, unavoidable moral problems. For instance, in a single-payer program like the one advocated for by Sanders, would abortion and contraception—birth control pills, birth control procedures, condoms, etc.—be paid for? According to Sanders, the answer is "yes."

In a separate section on his website about "Fighting for Women's Rights," Sanders' campaign stated:

Sen. Sanders has consistently fought against Republican attacks on the fundamental rights of women to control their own bodies. Sen. Sanders will fight to expand, not cut, funding for Planned Parenthood, the Title X family planning program, and other initiatives that protect women's health, access to contraception, and the availability of a safe and legal abortion.[34]

io/issues/medicare-for-all.

34   "Fighting for Women's Rights," berniesanders.com, accessed June 8, 2018, https://berniesanders.com/issues/fighting-for-womens-rights.

In a country in which the entire health insurance industry is socialized and the government pays for abortion and contraception, *all* taxpayers are required to pay for these services/products, including those taxpayers who believe such activities are extremely immoral. In the United States, numerous groups would fall into this category, but the one that often stands out among the rest, as I noted earlier in this book, is devout Roman Catholics.

In Roman Catholicism, both abortion and nearly all forms of contraception are forbidden by the Church's Magisterium—the Roman Catholic Church's authority on faith and moral issues. Those who knowingly and willingly use contraception, have an abortion, or encourage others to engage in these activities despite knowing such actions are considered "grave sins" are committing a "mortal sin"—a sin so severe that it's said to make shipwreck of a person's soul.

Requiring people to pay for contraception would force Roman Catholics, at least in part, to violate their beliefs. This is highly immoral, because no person in a free nation should be compelled to violate their sincerely held religious beliefs, and yet, this and other similar problems are inevitable in a socialized medical system.

Physician-Assisted Suicide

Contraception and abortion aren't the only moral controversies that arise when medical systems are socialized. Because health care, by definition, is deeply personal, it's impossible to separate religious beliefs and other ethical concerns from the wider system.

For instance, one of the most hotly debated moral issues in health care is whether patients suffering from illnesses that will eventually kill them should be permitted to commit "compassionate suicide," which requires assistance from a physician.

A 2015 Gallup survey found 68 percent of Americans support allowing physician-assisted suicide when "a person has a disease that cannot be cured and is living in severe pain," although only 56 percent said physician-assisted suicide is "morally acceptable."[35]

You might be tempted to think of physician-assisted suicide as a personal issue that doesn't affect anyone other than a dying patient and his or her family and doctor, but in a socialized medical system, everyone must participate in physician-assisted suicide, either directly or indirectly, because all taxpayers would be required to pay the physician and other health care workers involved. Taxpayers would also pay for the drugs used to kill the patient and for any materials given to the patient instructing him or her about physician-assisted suicide.

In a socialized medical system that permits suicide, it is, in a very real sense, the collective that kills the patient, not simply a single health care provider. The moral problems associated with such circumstances are apparent and deeply concerning for those who

---

35   Andrew Dugan, "In U.S., Support Up for Doctor-Assisted Suicide," Gallup, May 27, 2015, http://news.gallup.com/poll/183425/support-doctor-assisted-suicide.aspx.

believe physician-assisted suicide is morally wrong.

Socialized medical systems also put many doctors in difficult moral situations. If "health care is a right," as Sen. Sanders and others claim—and thus all people are entitled to abortion, physician-assisted suicide, and other controversial medical procedures—then what "rights" do medical providers have to choose not to perform these activities? What if a doctor's objections aren't based on religion but instead on non-religious, personal moral concerns? What if the collective decides doctors *must* perform abortions, physician-assisted suicides, etc.? What power would doctors have to say "no"? Could government regulations in socialized medical systems require hospitals to hire only those people who are willing to perform these procedures? Or perhaps only those doctors who agree to participate in the collective's mandates would get paid by the collective.

All these important moral concerns—and many more, too—only arise when an industry is socialized. In a truly free-market model, all health care providers have the power to voluntarily choose which procedures they feel most comfortable with, and no one is forced by law to engage in or pay for activities they have strong moral objections to.

Patients' Rights

Health care providers aren't the only ones who lose their ability to make important decisions in a socialist health care scheme. When health care is socialized, greater authority is granted to the collective, usually represented by the state, to make health care choices.

For instance, in countries with socialized medical systems, the collective decides whether to pay for elective health care costs for, say, an obese person, smokers, and drug users. In 2017, controversy arose when it was revealed some regions in the United Kingdom, which has a socialist medical system, planned to ration care by forcing people with a body mass index of 30 or higher and smokers to wait for at least a year for elective surgeries, a plan the head of the Royal College of Surgeons called "brutal" and the "most severe" policy "the modern [National Health Service] has ever seen."[36]

The bureaucrat advocating in favor of the policy explained, "Hospitals are being warned they will not be paid for surgery if they carry out operations on obese patients who are not exempt from the policy. This work will help to ensure that we get the very best value from the NHS and not exceed our resources or risk the ability of the NHS being there when people really need it."[37]

In socialized medicine, these kinds of rationing policies are common and likely unavoidable. When the collective makes health care choices, every personal health issue becomes inseparably linked to the ideas of the majority. So, if the majority decides it wants to compel obese people to lose weight, it can. If the majority decides

---

36   Hank Berrien, "Health Rationing In England: Obese And Smokers Banned From Routine Surgery," *The Daily Wire*, August 1, 2017, https://www.dailywire.com/news/19204/health-rationing-england-obese-and-smokers-banned-hank-berrien.

37   *Ibid.*

it doesn't want to cover the cost of back surgery on 80-year-old patients, it can. And, as the following case illustrates, if the majority decides some people's lives aren't worth living, it can do that as well.

In April 2018, Alfie Evans, a 23-month-old child, died in Alder Hey Children's Hospital in Liverpool, England. Prior to his death, Alfie's parents fought a lengthy legal battle to remove their son, who suffered from a degenerative neurological condition, from Alder Hey so they could bring Alfie to Rome for experimental treatments. The medical staff at Alder Hey determined Alfie's parents could not remove him from his hospital and that he should instead have his life support removed.[38]

The U.K. courts sided with Alder Hey and the government, eventually leading to Alfie's death. In the ruling issued by the United Kingdom's Supreme Court, the justices wrote it is "clear that parental rights are not absolute," and that existing laws "make it clear that when any question of the upbringing of a child comes before the courts, the child's welfare is the paramount consideration. As we explained in our earlier decision in this case, the best interests of the child are the 'gold standard' which is not only adopted by our law but also reflects the international standards to which this country is committed."

---

38   "Who was Alfie Evans and what was the row over his treatment?," BBC, April 28, 2018, https://www.bbc.com/news/uk-england-merseyside-43754949.

The justices then added:

It is therefore clear law that the parents do not have the right
to use the writ of habeas corpus to acquire the custody of their
child if this will not be in his best interests. The decisions of the
trial Judge clearly amount to decisions that the parents have no
right to direct Alfie's future medical treatment. This is not a criticism of them. How could it be? It simply means that they cannot
take Alfie away from Alder Hey for the purpose of transporting
him at some risk to other hospitals which can do him no good.

Here, the United Kingdom's socialist medical system, supported
by courts, determined it wouldn't be in the best interests of terminal-
ly ill Alfie Evans to allow his parents to attempt to save the young
boy's life. And upon what basis did the court determine this? The
claim that the collective, not Alfie's parents, have the ultimate power to decide what should happen to Alfie.

In all socialized industries, moral concerns must be determined
by the collective, leading to tragedies like the Alfie Evans case.
These problems aren't merely limited to socialized medical systems, but the life-and-death nature of health care makes these moral
problems more evident and reveals just how horrifying collective
decision-making can be.

Moral Forms of Socialism

Whether an entire nation's economy is socialized or simply a single industry, socialism is almost always accompanied by moral problems, which often lead to minority groups in society being compelled to participate in activities they are staunchly opposed to.

With that said, it *is* possible to build societies that include socialist programs that are arguably not immoral, but only if those programs deal exclusively with uncontroversial public services. For instance, most of America's roads are collectively owned, either at the local, state, or federal level, and, other than issues related to government fraud, waste, and abuse, there are few, if any, "public road controversies." The same is true with many public works projects, such as collectively owned water treatment plants or sewage systems.[39,40] (I'm not suggesting collective ownership of any industry is the most effective or efficient model. I'm simply pointing out that some socialized industries involve few moral controversies.)

Although these forms of socialism might be more morally ac-

---

39   Note that I'm not arguing collective ownership is the most effective way to manage public works projects—or anything else, for that matter. I'm limiting my comments here to issues relating only to morality.

40   Some pro-liberty, free-market advocates might argue that any form of collective ownership is immoral because in most forms, taxation is immoral. While I think most people agree excessive taxation is immoral, few Americans would likely argue all forms of taxation are immoral. My views on this matter are irrelevant for this work and have been omitted for the sake of brevity.

ceptable, few self-described socialists believe societies should limit themselves to socializing industries that deal only with uncontroversial issues. For example, I'm not aware of a single socialist party in the world that advocates for the privatization of the health care or health insurance industries. In fact, demanding some form of government-run health care is practically a prerequisite for calling oneself a "socialist."

5

Socialists' Objections Answered

In Chapters Three and Four, I went to great lengths to show why socialism is highly immoral, but it's important to remember that the people who advocate for these policies are often well-intentioned individuals who believe socialism is the best and perhaps only way to fix many of the world's most difficult crises.

I have spoken to numerous self-described socialists, and many more who closely associate themselves with liberalism or progressivism, and it's evident that many of these Americans truly believe socialist policies make the world a better place. In fact, some of the kindest and most generous people I know consider themselves part of the political Left. Openly declaring their left-wing ideology "evil" isn't done without great caution. Calling Marx's socialism "evil," however, is the most intellectually honest analysis I can deliver after carefully considering socialists' views and the logical implications of enacting socialist policies.

Below I briefly describe some of the most common objections I've heard, including from people whose opinions I greatly respect, to the moral concerns I've outlined in Chapters Three and Four and why I believe these objections don't hold up to scrutiny.

Objection: Socialism Is Superior to Capitalism

When faced with moral objections, some socialists react by insisting that whatever moral problems may exist if Marx's socialism is implemented, they would be far less severe than the serious issues facing capitalist countries around the world.

As I've noted repeatedly, little is gained by attempting to debate the effectiveness of Marxist socialist programs for a variety of reasons, including that a truly classless society has never been achieved anywhere in the world, making a debate on the effectiveness of such a scheme speculative. There is, however, nothing speculative about most of the moral concerns I've outlined in previous chapters.

Some might argue that even with socialism's moral problems, such a system would be far superior to the poverty we see in many market-based economies today. This claim, though, is riddled with assumptions.

For example, socialists making this argument assume their model will work without any historical evidence suggesting it would. It's very possible—and I would argue likely—their collective-property-ownership system, if fully implemented, would be a complete disaster, although I doubt such a model could ever exist because it seems to be in complete contradiction to human nature.

Another flawed aspect of this objection is that it attempts to compare problems related to the effectiveness of capitalism—especially poverty, wealth disparity, etc.—with the moral problems that *must* exist in a socialist scheme. It's entirely conceivable a capitalist, free-market economy in which all impoverished people are cared for because people charitably and voluntarily *choose* to help others could exist. Socialists might argue this has never happened and will never happen, but they can't argue it's impossible. And even the staunchest socialist must admit that the quality of life for impoverished people throughout the Western world has improved markedly over the past century, disproving many of the flawed predictions made by socialists more than a century ago, including Karl Marx. In many respects, the one-quarter of Americans with the least amount of wealth today live far better than some of the wealthiest Americans did a century ago, and much better than the "middle classes" of countless modern countries in Asia and Africa.

However unlikely it may seem to a socialist that people in a free-market society would take care of the sick and hungry by choice and not by coercion, they must acknowledge that it's at least possible. It is completely inconceivable, though, that a socialist country could avoid many of the moral pitfalls discussed earlier in this book, because collective property ownership, which is required in Marx's socialism, necessitates that the majority have total power over the minority to make all important moral decisions. Either a socialist agricultural society permits the killing of animals to feed its citizens, and thus forces some people who object to such activities to be part-owners of slaughterhouses, or it bans the killing of animals and prevents people who believe they have a natural right to hunt and fish from doing so. There is no other way.

Similarly, either a socialist society pays for contraception, and thus requires certain devout religious people to participate in activities they believe to be sinful, or it doesn't pay for contraception, angering feminists who believe contraception is a health care "right." Again, there can be no middle ground in socialized health care, because nearly all property in society or in a particular industry is owned and/or controlled collectively.

Objection: There's Nothing 'Evil' About Forcing People to Violate Their Deeply Held Moral Beliefs

Some socialists say that although their system might compel people to engage in activities they find abhorrent, if it's truly in their own best interests to do so, it shouldn't matter. In other words, moral concerns should always take a backseat to other societal problems.

There are several defects with this argument. One is that it has absolutely no objective standard upon which to base its claim. In other words, without a clear, unequivocal standard that can be used to show that lowering wealth disparity is more important than not violating the beliefs of various people, including religious groups, their view is, by definition, subjective and completely incapable of being proven.

It further assumes that all major religions throughout the entire world are false, because if any of those religions are true, then socialism doesn't merely force people to violate their beliefs, it compels all people to violate the will of God. Unless socialists can prove beyond a reasonable doubt all religions are false, they can't with any certainty say religious objections are less valuable than economic concerns. Surely, even reasonable atheistic socialists must admit that if they knew for certain God is real, His will for the world would need to supersede any attempts to impose "economic equality."

This objection from socialists also fails because socialists cannot prove economic concerns have a greater value than individual freedom, including religious liberty and the right to live freely without having to violate one's conscience. Socialists have a tendency to obsess over economic equality, but they almost always fail to assign any importance at all to freedom, which, as has been proven since the dawn of human history, has real and substantial *value* for most people. Who in America, for instance, would choose to live in a country where they have all the food, health care, education, and shelter they could ever need, but no ability to speak, worship, receive a fair trial, or think freely? Americans, as well as many people around the world, value their personal freedom more than many economic concerns, and without presenting a strong reason for why they are wrong, this socialist objection carries little weight.

Objection: Total Uniformity Is Possible

When I presented some of my concerns about whether it's possible for socialism to coexist with religious liberty, The Socialist Party of Great Britain (SPGB) responded to me on Twitter with the following message: "As socialist consciousness becomes far more widespread, this will most probably be accompanied by a growing decline in the need for religion." Along with that message was a picture of Karl Marx and a caption that read, "Religion is the impotence of the human mind to deal with occurrences it cannot understand."

I found this response surprisingly refreshing and honest. Rather than fabricate an unlikely fictional scenario in which Marxist socialism could exist with religious liberty, The Socialist Party of Great Britain simply appeared to acknowledge that the two ideas are incompatible.

If you're puzzled a bit by SPGB's response, it's worth mentioning it fits quite well with many other statements made by Marx and other socialists of the nineteenth century. Generally speaking, many (but not all) socialists of that era believed religion is a tool used by wealthier classes to control working-class people.

In *The Communist Manifesto*, Marx wrote:

"Undoubtedly," it will be said, "religious, moral, philosophical and juridical ideas have been modified in the course of historical development. But religion, morality philosophy, political science, and law, constantly survived this change."

"There are, besides, eternal truths, such as Freedom, Justice, etc. that are common to all states of society. But Communism abolishes eternal truths, it abolishes all religion, and all morality, instead of constituting them on a new basis; it therefore acts in contradiction to all past historical experience."

What does this accusation reduce itself to? The history of all past society has consisted in the development of class antagonisms, antagonisms that assumed different forms at different epochs.

But whatever form they may have taken, one fact is common to all past ages, viz., the exploitation of one part of society by the other. No wonder, then, that the social consciousness of past ages, despite all the multiplicity and variety it displays, moves within certain common forms, or general ideas, which cannot completely vanish except with the total disappearance of class antagonisms.

The Communist revolution is the most radical rupture with traditional property relations; no wonder that its development involves the most radical rupture with traditional ideas.[41]

In Marx's introduction to *A Contribution to the Critique of Hegel's Philosophy of Right*, he wrote perhaps his most well-known passage on religion:

Religious distress is at the same time the expression of real distress and also the protest against real distress. Religion is the sigh of the oppressed creature, the heart of a heartless world, just as it is the spirit of spiritless conditions. It is the opium of the people.

To abolish religion as the illusory happiness of the people is to demand their real happiness. The demand to give up illusions about the existing state of affairs is the demand to give up a state of affairs which needs illusions. The criticism of religion is therefore in embryo the criticism of the vale of tears, the halo of which is religion.

Criticism has torn up the imaginary flowers from the chain not so that man shall wear the unadorned, bleak chain but so that he will shake off the chain and pluck the living flower. The criticism of religion disillusions man to make him think and act

---

41   Karl Marx, *supra* note 1, pp. 19–20.

and shape his reality like a man who has been disillusioned and has come to reason, so that he will revolve round himself and therefore round his true sun. Religion is only the illusory sun which revolves round man as long as he does not revolve round himself.[42]

Marx, as well as other socialists, seem to believe religion will likely, at least to some extent, disappear with the coming socialist-communist revolution, making some of the moral concerns I've outlined throughout much of this book irrelevant. If there were no religions, then obviously there would be no controversies regarding nuns and contraception or Hindus and the killing of cows. But Marxists often don't stop there. They believe that because most struggles result from class "antagonisms" created by wealthier classes, most moral disagreements would fade away if private property were to be owned collectively, as Marx noted in *The Communist Manifesto*:

National differences and antagonisms between peoples are daily more and more vanishing, owing to the development of the bourgeoisie, to freedom of commerce, to the world-market, to uniformity in the mode of production and in the conditions

42   Karl Marx, "Introduction," *A Contribution to the Critique of Hegel's Philosophy of Right*, first published in *Deutsch-Französische Jahrbücher* on February 7, 1844 in Paris, France. Made available online by marxists.org, accessed June 8, 2018, https://www.marxists.org/archive/marx/works/1843/critique-hpr/intro.htm.

of life corresponding thereto.

The supremacy of the proletariat will cause them to vanish still faster. United action, of the leading civilised countries at least, is one of the first conditions for the emancipation of the proletariat. In proportion as the exploitation of one individual by another is put an end to, the exploitation of one nation by another will also be put an end to.

In proportion as the antagonism between classes within the nation vanishes, the hostility of one nation to another will come to an end.[43]

My personal religious views compel me to believe that religion will not fade entirely from the Earth, as many Marxists suggest, but history is equally persuasive. Religion has seemingly always existed among humans, and to suggest religious beliefs will suddenly vanish seems quite foolish and contradictory to the entire history of civilization.

Even if religion were to disappear, however, that doesn't mean all people would suddenly agree on every important moral issue. Few non-religious people hold identical positions on every moral controversy today, and I'm not sure why the rise of socialism would change that reality. In fact, throughout my study of socialism, it's

---

43   Karl Marx, *supra* note 1, pp. 18–19.

become clear that there are a number of disagreements within the modern socialist movement, too. If socialists can't even agree on every moral issue, why would they believe the entirety of the world would do so?

Again, as with other socialist objections, it seems socialists are more than willing to offer speculation but can't provide any support for their radical predictions for the future. People have and always will hold diverse opinions on a wide range of issues, and no amount of wishing by socialists will change that.

Conclusion

Despite its utopian promises of a classless, harmonious, democratic society, socialism, even if implemented to Marx's standards, either requires all people to abandon their personal morals in favor of some unknown universal standard of morality—something that has never come remotely close to occurring—or some people must participate in social programs or activities that violate their beliefs. Socialism offers no other alternatives, because the collective ownership and control of property gives power to the majority to impose their morals on minorities. In fact, it mandates such an arrangement.

Marx's socialism cannot be adopted without these moral problems, and the mixed-socialist economies of Europe present substantial, albeit less serious, moral problems of their own.

Only those societies that place far more value on limiting wealth disparities than they do on individual liberty, freedom of conscience,

and religious freedom can adopt socialism, assuming it's even possible for Marx's democratic socialism to take root. There are strong
reasons to believe socialism has never existed to its fullest extent
because it violates essential and incontrovertible aspects of human
nature.

Whatever problems exist in a capitalist society, they pale in
comparison to the moral tragedies that *must* accompany Marx's socialism, which is why it should be avoided at all costs. To do other-
wise would be to perpetrate a great injustice on the free peoples of
the world.

Notes

1. Karl Marx, *The Communist Manifesto*, Amazon Digital Services, Kindle Edition, n.d., pp. 13–14, ASIN: B00MJJ7YZE.

2. "What Is Socialism?," The Socialist Party of Great Britain, accessed May 25, 2018, https://www.worldsocialism.org/spgb/what-socialism.

3. Karl Marx, *supra* note 1, p. 13.

4. Note that not all socialists agree that there shouldn't be markets. Some believe markets can operate within a socialist model, but only if all the means of production (all industry) is collectively owned.

5. The Socialist Party of Great Britain, *supra* note 2.

6. "Socialism As Radical Democracy: Statement of Principles of the Socialist Party USA," Socialist Party USA, accessed May 25, 2018, https://www.socialistpartyusa.net/principles-points-of-

agreement.

7.   "Where We Stand: Building the Next Left," Democratic Socialists of America, accessed May 25, 2018, http://www.dsausa.org/where_ we_stand#dc.

8.   "Our Object and Declaration of Principles," The Socialist Party of Great Britain, originally published in 1904, accessed May 25, 2018, https://www.worldsocialism.org/spgb/our-object-and-declaration-principles.

9.   In Marx's writings, the "proletariat" is essentially the global "working class" in society—those who produce the world's food, buildings, machinery, etc. with their labor.

10.   In Marx's writings, the "bourgeois" is the economic ruling class in society—those who control most of the world's capital. It's better not to think of these individuals as royalty or even as the world's wealthiest people, but rather as the relatively large group, although still much smaller than the working class, in society that controls the overwhelming majority of the industries.

11.   Karl Marx, *supra* note 1, pp. 18–19.

12.   *Ibid.*, pp. 20–21.

13.   Adam Buick, "A Question of Definition: (4) Socialism/ Communism," *Socialist Standard*, Issue 886, June 1978, https:// www.worldsocialism.org/spgb/socialist-standard/1970s/1978/no-886-june-1978/question-definition-4-socialismcommunism.

14.   *Ibid.*

15.   *Ibid.*

16. David Gilmour, "What Is Socialism, Really?," *The Daily Dot*, June 28, 2017, https://www.dailydot.com/layer8/what-is-socialism-definition/.

17. Adam Buick, *supra* note 13.

18. *Ibid.*

19. *Ibid.*

20. Robert Frank, "Richest 1% now owns half the world's wealth," CNBC.com, November 14, 2017, https://www.cnbc.com/2017/11/14/richest-1-percent-now-own-half-the-worlds-wealth.html.

21. *Global Wealth Report 2017*, Credit Suisse Research, 2017, http://publications.credit-suisse.com/tasks/render/file/index.cfm?fileid=12DFFD63-07D1-EC63-A3D5F67356880EF3.

22. Wendy Doniger, "Hinduism and its complicated history with cows (and people who eat them)," *The Conversation*, July 16, 2017, http://theconversation.com/hinduism-and-its-complicated-history-with-cows-and-people-who-eat-them-80586.

23. See Quran 5:3.

24. "Why do Muslims abstain from pork?," WhyIslam.org, August 9, 2011, https://www.whyislam.org/faqs/restrictions-in-islam/why-do-muslims-abstain-from-pork.

25. Book of Leviticus 11:7–8, New International Version of the Bible.

26. "Why Animal Rights?," People for the Ethical Treatment of Animals, accessed June 5, 2018, https://www.peta.org/about-peta/why-peta/why-animal-rights.

27. "Global Views on Morality," Pew Research Center, 2014, accessed June 7, 2018, http://www.pewglobal.org/2014/04/15/global-morality.

28. "Gambling," lds.org, Church of Jesus Christ of Latter-Day Saints, accessed June 7, 2018, https://www.lds.org/topics/gambling?lang=eng.

29. Pew Research Center, *supra* note 27.

30. Karl Marx, *supra* note 1, p. 18.

31. *Ibid.*, pp. 18–19.

32. Karl Marx, *supra* note 1, p. 21.

33. "Medicare for All: Leaving No One Behind," berniesanders. com, accessed June 8, 2018, https://live-berniesanders-com. pantheonsite.io/issues/medicare-for-all.

34. "Fighting for Women's Rights," berniesanders.com, accessed June 8, 2018, https://berniesanders.com/issues/fighting-for-womens-rights.

35. Andrew Dugan, "In U.S., Support Up for Doctor-Assisted Suicide," Gallup, May 27, 2015, http://news.gallup.com/poll/183425/support-doctor-assisted-suicide.aspx.

36. Hank Berrien, "Health Rationing In England: Obese And Smokers Banned From Routine Surgery," *The Daily Wire*, August 1, 2017, https://www.dailywire.com/news/19204/health-rationing-england-obese-and-smokers-banned-hank-berrien.

37. *Ibid.*

38. "Who was Alfie Evans and what was the row over his treatment?,"

BBC, April 28, 2018, https://www.bbc.com/news/uk-england-merseyside-43754949.

39. Note that I'm not arguing collective ownership is the most effective way to manage public works projects—or anything else, for that matter. I'm limiting my comments here to issues relating only to morality.

40. Some pro-liberty, free-market advocates might argue that any form of collective ownership is immoral because in most forms, taxation is immoral. While I think most people agree excessive taxation is immoral, few Americans would likely argue all forms of taxation are immoral. My views on this matter are irrelevant for this work and have been omitted for the sake of brevity.

41. Karl Marx, *supra* note 1, pp. 19–20.

42. Karl Marx, "Introduction," *A Contribution to the Critique of Hegel's Philosophy of Right*, first published in *Deutsch-Französische Jahrbücher* on February 7, 1844, in Paris, France. Made available online by marxists.org, accessed June 8, 2018, https://www.marxists.org/archive/marx/works/1843/critique-hpr/intro.htm.

43. Karl Marx, *supra* note 1, pp. 18–19.

About the Author

Justin Haskins is senior editor and a research fellow at The Henry Dearborn Institute for Liberty, an association of pro-liberty professionals and scholars, and executive editor and a research fellow at a free-market think tank.

Haskins has been published hundreds of times in various media outlets, including *The Wall Street Journal*, *New York Post*, *Forbes*, *Newsweek*, FoxNews.com, *U.S. News and World Report*, and *National Review*, among many others. Haskins currently serves as a frequent contributor for *The Hill*, *Washington Examiner*, and *The Blaze*. He's also a columnist for Townhall.com, where he writes a weekly column about culture and public policy controversies.

Haskins' work has been featured by the Fox News Channel, *New York Times*, *Drudge Report*, Newsmax TV, NRA TV, *Real Clear Politics*, the White House, and the *Rush Limbaugh Show*.

In 2016, Haskins was named to MediaDC's "30 Under 30" list of young and influential leaders on the right, and in 2017, Newsmax named Haskins one of the nation's "Top 30 Republicans Under 30." Haskins was inducted into The Philadelphia Society in 2018.

Haskins earned his bachelor's degree from the University of Richmond in 2010, and he received a master's degree in government from Regent University (Virginia Beach, VA) in 2011. In 2015, Haskins earned a second master's degree, this time in journalism, from Regent University.

Haskins, a native of New Hampshire, currently splits his time living in New England and North Carolina with his wife, Dr. Jacquelyn, and his pro-liberty dog Roxy.

Made in the USA
Lexington, KY
27 October 2019